1 Batter—50

Baking to Fit Your Every Occasion

Contents

Fundamentals

Recipes

Appendix

Just Desserts

Tart dough or cake batter, yeast dough or butter cake—it seems like you need a different batter for every dessert. Wouldn't it be nice if there was just one basic batter that could be used for all kinds of cakes and tortes, that was made from ingredients you always have on hand? One that could be prepared in a jiffy, that would always succeed, and that you would know by heart after making it only a couple times?

That batter is here!

The following pages contain 50 varieties of cake, and soon you'll be coming up with your own creations based on this basic batter.

Basic Recipe

Ingredients

You can use any neutral-tasting oil but because of high baking temperatures, be sure to use refined oils or oils with a high smoking point (not cold-pressed). For liquids, you can use juice, dairy, coffee, or wine. The other ingredients you'll add for flavoring—for example, spices, cocoa powder, chocolate, and nuts—are described in the individual recipes.

Basic Batter

FOR ONE 11-INCH SPRING-FORM PAN, ONE 13-INCH LOAF PAN OR ONE 10- X 15-INCH JELLYROLL PAN

➤ **4 medium eggs**
  1¼ cups sugar
  ¾ cup oil
  ¾ cup liquid (liquid will vary depending on the recipe)
  2¼ cups flour
  1 tbs baking powder

NOTES

Grease pans well and sprinkle with flour. In the case of springform pans, grease and sprinkle only the bottom so the batter will be able to "climb" the sides.

Never fill pans more than two-thirds full because the batter will rise while baking.

In an oven with more than three possible rack heights, "the bottom rack" means second rack from the bottom.

1 Preheat oven to 400°F. Measure out all the ingredients exactly according to the recipe and keep them within reach on the work surface.

2 Beat eggs and sugar in a mixing bowl for 2–3 minutes until light and creamy. Add oil and liquid to sugar and egg mixture while stirring constantly.

3 Sift flour, combine with baking powder, and add to remaining ingredients. Pour batter into the prepared pan (see Tips) and bake in the oven for 25 minutes (bottom rack) in a shallow pan or 45 minutes in a deep pan. Do the chopstick test (page 65)!

Tools

For the batter: To measure ingredients accurately, you'll need a set of measuring cups in ¼ cup units. Always remember to level cup and tbs/tsp measurements when possible. It's easiest to stir the batter with an electric hand mixer, and the best way to get all the batter out of the bowl is with a rubber spatula.

For baking: Black plated pans are ideal for electric ovens because they're good at reflecting the heat back onto the contents, helping the cake brown well.

In this book, we use an 11-inch springform and an 11-inch tube (or Angel Food) pan made of this material.

For baking: Tinplate and aluminum pans are also excellent conductors of heat but require more heat than black plated pans, making them ideal for gas ovens.

For baking: Nonstick cake pans are especially practical because it's easy to remove the finished cake and the pans are easy to clean.

In this book, we use a 9-inch (or 10-cup) Bundt pan and a 13-inch loaf pan.

For baking: Jellyroll pans have extra high sides and are ideal for all types of sheet cakes. Or you can use the broiler pan from the oven.

In this book we use a 10- x 15-inch jellyroll pan and a 12- x 18-inch deep baking sheet.

For the finishing touches: You'll need a tart ring (an adjustable metal or plastic ring placed around the cake base) for all cakes with a liquid filling or topping. You'll also need a pastry bag with a star tip if you want to decorate your tortes and cakes. With a little practice, you'll have them looking like they came from a professional bakery in no time!

Chocolate, Nuts, Etc.

Even novice bakers will be able to make these cakes. They're easy as can be and super fast! They are flavored with such extras as walnuts, hazelnuts, almonds, chocolate, poppy seeds, citrus extracts, wine, and spices.

Quick Recipes

Nut Cake

MAKES 1 TUBE PAN (20 PIECES):

➤ For the cake:
   4 eggs | $1^1/_4$ cups sugar | $^3/_4$ cup oil
   $^3/_4$ cup milk | $1^1/_4$ cups ground hazelnuts
   $2^1/_4$ cups flour | 1 tbs baking powder
➤ For the glaze:
   3 tbs hazelnut paste (can substitute
   1 tbs hazelnut extract) | $^1/_4$ cup sugar
   $^1/_4$ cup water | 20 whole hazelnuts

1 | Preheat oven to 400°F. Beat eggs and sugar
until light and creamy. Add oil and milk.
Briskly stir in ground nuts and flour mixed
with baking powder.

2 | Pour batter into prepared pan and bake in
oven (bottom rack) for 40–45 minutes.

3 | Meanwhile, melt hazelnut paste and sugar
in water until thick enough to coat a spoon.
Spread cooled cake with hazelnut glaze and
decorate with whole hazelnuts.

Chocolate Cake

MAKES 1 LOAF PAN (15 PIECES):

➤ 4 eggs | $1^1/_4$ cups sugar | $^3/_4$ cup oil
   $^3/_4$ cup orange juice | $2^1/_4$ cups flour
   1 tbs baking powder
   3 tbs cocoa powder
   $1^1/_4$ cups semisweet chocolate
   couverture

1 | Preheat oven to 400°F. Beat eggs and
sugar until light and creamy. Add oil
and juice. Briskly stir in flour mixed
with baking powder and cocoa powder.

2 | Pour batter into prepared pan and
bake in the oven (bottom rack) for 40–45
minutes. Then let cool and spread cake
with melted semisweet chocolate.

7

Traditional with
a New Twist

Trio Swirl

MAKES 1 BUNDT PAN:

➤ **4 eggs**
1¼ cups sugar
¾ cup oil
¾ cup orange juice
2¼ cups flour
1 tbs baking powder
2 tbs cocoa powder
5 tbs ground hazelnuts
Powdered sugar for dusting

🕐 Prep time: 20 minutes
🕐 Baking time: 60 minutes
➤ Calories per piece (16): About 240

1 | Preheat oven to 400°F.

2 | Beat eggs and sugar until light and creamy. Add oil and juice. Briskly stir in flour mixed with baking powder. Pour one-third of the batter into the prepared pan.

3 | Divide remaining batter in half. Stir cocoa into one half and pour into pan along the outside edge.

4 | Stir ground hazelnuts into final third of batter. Carefully pour this batter along the inside of the Bundt pan.

5 | Bake cake in the oven (bottom rack) for 50–60 minutes, let cool, and serve dusted with powdered sugar.

Moist | Portable

Carrot Cake

MAKES 1 LOAF PAN:

➤ **4 eggs**
1¼ cups sugar
¾ cup oil
¾ cup sweetened carrot juice
½ cup grated carrots
1¼ cups ground hazelnuts
2¼ cups flour
1 tbs baking powder
➤ **For the glaze and decorations:**
1 cup powdered sugar
Juice from ½ lemon
6 marzipan carrots

🕐 Prep time: 25 minutes
🕐 Baking time: 50 minutes
➤ Calories per piece (15): About 340

1 | Preheat oven to 400°F.

2 | Beat eggs and sugar until light and creamy. Add oil and juice. Briskly stir in carrots, hazelnuts, and flour mixed with baking powder.

3 | Pour batter into prepared pan and bake in the oven (bottom rack) for 50 minutes. Let cool.

4 | Sift powdered sugar and stir in lemon juice drop by drop to make a smooth, syrupy glaze. Spread onto cake, arrange marzipan carrots on top, and let the glaze dry.

TIP Wrap this cake in plastic wrap and it will stay fresh and moist for quite a while!

Fast | Inexpensive
Lemon Cake

MAKES 1 BUNDT PAN:

➤ 2 1/2 lemons
4 eggs
1 1/4 cups sugar
3/4 cup oil
1/4 cup orange juice
2 1/4 cups flour
1 tbs baking powder
1 cup powdered sugar

🕐 Prep time: 25 minutes
🕐 Baking time: 55 minutes
➤ Calories per piece (16):
About 235

1 | Preheat oven to 400°F. Remove zest from one lemon and squeeze juice from all of the lemons. Beat eggs and sugar until light and creamy. Add oil, orange juice, and 3/4 of the lemon juice. Briskly stir in half of the lemon zest, flour, and baking powder. Pour batter into prepared pan and bake in the oven (bottom rack) for 50–55 minutes.

2 | Sift powdered sugar and mix with remaining lemon juice to make a smooth glaze. Spread onto cake and sprinkle with remaining lemon zest.

Traditional with a New Twist
Marble Cake

MAKES 1 BUNDT PAN:

➤ 4 eggs
1 1/4 cups sugar
3/4 cup oil
3/4 cup orange juice
2 1/4 cups flour
1 tbs baking powder
1/4 cup poppy seeds
1/2 cup raisins
1 tsp cinnamon
1 1/4 cups powdered sugar
4 tbs rum (or orange juice)

🕐 Prep time: 30 minutes
🕐 Baking time: 60 minutes
➤ Calories per piece (16):
About 290

1 | Preheat oven to 400°F. Beat eggs and sugar until light and creamy. Add oil and juice, then stir in flour mixed with baking powder. Pour half the batter into the prepared pan. Combine other half with poppy seeds, raisins, and 1/2 tsp cinnamon and pour into pan along the outside edge. Bake cake in the oven (bottom rack) for 50–60 minutes.

2 | Mix powdered sugar, remaining cinnamon, and rum to make a glaze. Use to frost cooled cake.

Easy | For Company
Coffee Ring

MAKES 1 TUBE PAN:

➤ 4 eggs
1 1/4 cups sugar
3/4 cup oil
1 cup cold espresso
3/4 cup chopped almonds
1/2 cup grated chocolate
1 pinch ground cardamom
Zest from 1 orange
2 1/4 cups flour
1 tbs baking powder
1 1/4 cups powdered sugar
Chocolate-covered espresso beans

🕐 Prep time: 25 minutes
🕐 Baking time: 50 minutes
➤ Calories per piece (20):
About 245

1 | Preheat oven to 400°F. Beat eggs and sugar until light and creamy. Add oil, 3/4 cup espresso, and all other ingredients except powdered sugar and espresso beans. Pour batter into prepared pan and bake in the oven (bottom rack) for 50 minutes.

2 | Sift powdered sugar and mix with remaining espresso to make a smooth glaze. Use to frost cake and then decorate with chocolate-covered espresso beans.

Traditional | Fast

Red Wine Cake

MAKES 1 BUNDT PAN:

- ➤ 4 eggs
  1¼ cups sugar
  ¾ cup oil
  ¾ cup red wine
  ¾ cup ground hazelnuts
  1 cup grated chocolate
  2¼ cups flour
  1 tbs baking powder
  1 tbs cinnamon
  1¼ cups semisweet
  chocolate couverture

- ⏱ Prep time: 20 minutes
- ⏱ Baking time: 60 minutes
- ➤ Calories per piece (16):
  About 355

1 | Preheat oven to 400°F.
Beat eggs and sugar until
light and creamy. Add oil and
wine. Briskly stir in hazelnuts,
grated chocolate, and flour
mixed with baking powder
and cinnamon.

2 | Pour batter into prepared
pan and bake in the oven
(bottom rack) for 60 minutes.

3 | Melt couverture in a
double boiler and use to
frost cooled cake.

Aromatic

Allspice Cake

MAKES 1 SPRINGFORM PAN:

- ➤ 1 cup walnuts
  4 eggs
  1¼ cups sugar
  ¾ cup oil
  ¾ cup orange juice
  ¼ cup chopped candied
  orange peel
  2¼ cups flour
  1 tbs baking powder
  2 tbs cocoa powder
  2 tbs allspice
- ➤ For the glaze and
  decorations:
  1¼ cups powdered sugar
  1 pinch allspice
  2 tbs rum (may substitute
  orange juice)
  About 32 walnut halves
  2 tbs chopped candied
  orange peel

- ⏱ Prep time: 40 minutes
- ⏱ Baking time: 45 minutes
- ➤ Calories per piece (12):
  About 450

1 | Preheat oven to 400°F.
Chop walnuts for the batter.
Beat eggs and sugar until light
and creamy. Add oil and juice,
then stir in walnuts and
candied orange peel. Briskly

stir in flour mixed with
baking powder, cocoa
powder, and allspice.

2 | Pour batter into prepared
pan, bake in the oven
(bottom rack) for 40–45
minutes, and let cool.

3 | Sift together powdered
sugar and allspice and stir in
rum drop by drop to make
a smooth, syrupy glaze.
Distribute glaze on cake, then
decorate with walnut halves,
sprinkle with candied orange
peel, and let glaze dry.

TIP It looks fantastic if you
dip some of the walnut
halves into melted
chocolate couverture
before putting them
on the cake.

A World of Fruit

Stirred together in a flash and wonderfully moist, made with either fresh, seasonal fruit or something out of a can—it doesn't have to be summer for you to feast your eyes and taste buds on these cakes!

Quick Recipes

Currant Cake

MAKES 1 SPRINGFORM PAN
(12 PIECES):

➤ 4 eggs | $1^1/_4$ cups sugar | $^3/_4$ cup oil
$^3/_4$ cup orange juice | $2^1/_4$ cups flour
1 tbs baking powder
2 tbs cocoa powder
2 cups dried red currants

1 | Preheat oven to 400°F. Beat eggs and
sugar until light and creamy. Add oil and
juice. Briskly stir in flour mixed with
baking powder. Divide batter in half.
Stir cocoa into one half and add to the
prepared pan. Bake this half in the oven
(bottom rack) for 15 minutes.

2 | Fold currants into remaining batter
and distribute over prebaked base. Bake
cake for 25 more minutes.

Banana Cake

FOR 1 TUBE PAN (20 PIECES):

➤ 1 large banana | 2 tsp lemon juice
4 eggs | $1^1/_4$ cups sugar
$^3/_4$ cup oil | $^3/_4$ cup banana puree
$^3/_4$ cup ground hazelnuts
$^1/_2$ tsp ground ginger
$2^1/_4$ cups flour
1 tbs baking powder

1 | Preheat oven to 400°F. Peel bananas,
mash, and combine with lemon juice.

2 | Beat eggs and sugar until light and
creamy. Add oil. Stir in banana purée,
nuts, and ginger. Briskly stir in flour
mixed with baking powder. Pour batter
into prepared pan and bake in the oven
(bottom rack) for 45–50 minutes.

Fast | Moist

Tangerine Cake

MAKES 1 TUBE PAN:

- ➤ **4 eggs**
  1¼ cups sugar
  ¾ cup oil
  ¾ cup orange juice
  2¼ cups flour
  1 tbs baking powder
  3 tangerines, peeled
- ➤ **For the glaze and**
  decorations:
  1¾ cups powdered sugar
  Juice from 1 lemon
  3 tbs chopped pistachios

- 🕐 Prep time: 20 minutes
- 🕐 Baking time: 50 minutes
- ➤ Calories per piece (20):
  About 215

1 | Preheat oven to 400°F. Beat eggs and sugar until light and creamy. Add oil and juice. Briskly stir in flour mixed with baking powder. Pour batter into prepared pan and prebake in the oven (bottom rack) for 5–10 minutes. Arrange tangerine sections on top, bake cake for another 35–40 minutes, and let cool.

2 | Sift powdered sugar and stir in lemon juice drop by drop to make a smooth, syrupy glaze. Distribute over cake and sprinkle with chopped pistachios. Let glaze dry.

For Company | Fruity

Rhubarb Poppy Seed Cake

MAKES 1 SPRINGFORM PAN:

- ➤ **4–5 stalks rhubarb**
  4 eggs
  1¼ cups sugar
  ¾ cup oil
  ¾ cup orange juice
  2¼ cups flour
  1 tbs baking powder
  ¼ cup poppy seeds
  ¼ cup sliced almonds
  1 pinch ground coriander
  Powdered sugar for
  dusting

- 🕐 Prep time: 30 minutes
- 🕐 Baking time: 50 minutes
- ➤ Calories per piece (12):
  About 330

1 | Preheat oven to 400°F. Clean rhubarb, peel, and cut into small pieces.

2 | Beat eggs and sugar until light and creamy. Add oil and juice. Briskly stir in flour mixed with baking powder. Pour half the batter into prepared pan and prebake in the oven (bottom rack) for 15 minutes.

3 | Thoroughly mix together remaining batter with poppy seeds, almonds, coriander, and rhubarb pieces and distribute over prebaked base. Bake cake for another 30–35 minutes. Serve dusted with powder sugar.

 TIP Goes well with almond whipped cream (recipe on page 59).

Best when Fresh
Apricot Cake

MAKES 1 SPRINGFORM PAN:

- 1 (16-oz) can apricots
  4 eggs
  $1\frac{1}{4}$ cups sugar
  $\frac{3}{4}$ cup oil
  4 cups flour
  1 tbs baking powder
  3 tsp cocoa powder
  $\frac{1}{2}$ cup butter
  1 tsp vanilla

- Prep time: 35 minutes
- Baking time: 50 minutes
- Calories per piece (12):
  About 480

1 | Preheat oven to 400°F. Drain apricots and set aside about $\frac{3}{4}$ cup juice. Beat eggs and 1 cup sugar until light and creamy. Stir in oil, juice, 2 cups flour, baking powder, and cocoa powder. In the prepared pan, prebake half the batter in the oven (bottom rack) for 15 minutes.

2 | Melt butter and mix with vanilla, remaining sugar, and flour to make a streusel. Place apricots on prebaked batter and then cover with remaining batter. Distribute streusel on top and bake cake for another 30–35 minutes.

Impressive | Fast
Blackberry Tart

MAKES 1 SPRINGFORM PAN:

- 2 pints blackberries
  4 eggs
  $\frac{2}{3}$ cup sugar
  $\frac{1}{2}$ cup oil
  $\frac{1}{2}$ cup buttermilk
  $1\frac{1}{2}$ cups flour
  $1\frac{1}{2}$ tsp baking powder
  $\frac{3}{4}$ cup marzipan (4 oz)
  $\frac{3}{4}$ cup sour cream

- Prep time: 25 minutes
- Baking time: 35 minutes
- Calories per piece (12):
  About 225

1 | Preheat oven to 400°F. Rinse berries and drain. Beat 2 eggs and sugar until light and creamy. Add oil and buttermilk. Briskly stir in flour mixed with baking powder. Pour batter into prepared pan and prebake in the oven (bottom rack) for 10 minutes.

2 | Beat 2 eggs and marzipan until foamy. Stir in sour cream. Arrange blackberries on prebaked base, pour egg mixture over the top, and bake cake for another 20–25 minutes.

Aromatic | Moist
Plum Nut Cake

MAKES 1 LOAF PAN:

- 3–4 plums
  1 cup walnuts
  4 eggs
  $1\frac{1}{4}$ cups sugar
  $\frac{3}{4}$ cup oil
  $\frac{3}{4}$ cup orange juice
  $\frac{1}{2}$ cup ground almonds
  1 heaping tsp cinnamon
  $2\frac{1}{4}$ cups flour
  1 tbs baking powder
  $1\frac{1}{4}$ cups powdered sugar
  2 tsp rum (or orange juice)

- Prep time: 35 minutes
- Baking time: 60 minutes
- Calories per piece (15):
  About 360

1 | Preheat oven to 400°F. Rinse plums, remove pits, and dice. Chop walnuts. Beat eggs and sugar until light and creamy. Add oil, juice, all the nuts, 1 level tsp cinnamon, and flour mixed with baking powder. Fold in plums. Pour batter into prepared pan and bake in the oven (bottom rack) for 50–60 minutes.

2 | Stir together powdered sugar, remaining cinnamon, and rum to make a glaze and spread over cooled cake.

Can Prepare in Advance

Apple Cake

MAKES 1 SPRINGFORM PAN:

- 4 eggs
  - $1^1/_4$ cups sugar
  - $^3/_4$ cup oil
  - $^3/_4$ cup apple juice
  - 1 cup ground hazelnuts
  - $^1/_4$ cup chopped almonds
  - $2^1/_4$ cups flour
  - 1 tbs baking powder
  - 1 tsp ground star anise
- For the topping:
  - $1^1/_4$ sticks butter
  - 3 tbs sugar
  - $^1/_2$ tsp cinnamon
  - $1^1/_2$ cups flour
  - 3 large apples
  - Powdered sugar
  - for dusting

🕒 Prep time: 40 minutes

🕒 Baking time: 60 minutes

➤ Calories per piece (12):
  About 575

1 | Preheat oven to 400°F. Beat eggs and sugar until light and creamy. Add oil and juice. Briskly stir in hazelnuts, almonds, flour mixed with baking powder, and star anise. Pour batter into prepared pan and prebake in the oven (bottom rack) for 15 minutes.

2 | Melt butter and mix with sugar, cinnamon, and flour to make a crumbly dough. Peel apples, cut into quarters, remove cores, and cut wedges crosswise into fine slices. Arrange on the cake, top with streusel, and bake cake for another 45 minutes. Serve dusted with powdered sugar.

For Company | Aromatic

Covered Pear Cake

MAKES 1 SPRINGFORM PAN:

- 4 eggs
  - $1^1/_4$ cups sugar
  - $^3/_4$ cup oil
  - $^3/_4$ cup milk
  - $2^1/_4$ cups flour
  - 4 tsp rolled oats
  - 1 tsp baking powder
  - 1 tbs cocoa powder
  - $^1/_2$ tsp cinnamon
  - 1 pinch ground nutmeg
  - 2 pears
  - Powdered sugar for dusting

🕒 Prep time: 30 minutes

🕒 Baking time: 50 minutes

➤ Calories per piece (12):
  About 315

1 | Preheat oven to 400°F. Beat eggs and sugar until light and creamy. Add oil and milk. Briskly stir in flour, oats, baking powder, cocoa powder, and spices. Pour half the batter into prepared pan and prebake in the oven (bottom rack) for 15 minutes.

2 | Peel pears, cut into quarters, and remove cores. Cut wedges crosswise into fine slices, arrange on the prebaked base, and cover with remaining batter. Bake pear cake for another 30–35 minutes. Serve dusted with powdered sugar.

TIP

Decorating
This cake also tastes delicious covered with a chocolate glaze and sprinkled with whole or chopped pistachios.

Bars, Brownies, and More

These cakes are not only fast but yield a large number of servings—ideal when you're expecting a crowd for coffee! You'll find many fresh, fruity, and nutty bar cookies along with some non-traditional brownies.

Quick Recipes

Blueberry Cake

MAKES 1 JELLYROLL PAN (15 PIECES):

➤ 4 eggs | 1¼ cups sugar | ¾ cup oil
¾ cup orange juice | 2¼ cups flour
1 tbs baking powder
1½ pints blueberries
1½ cups powdered sugar
Juice from 1 lemon

1 | Preheat oven to 400°F. Beat eggs and
sugar until light and creamy. Add oil, juice,
and flour mixed with baking powder.
Spread out batter in the prepared pan and
prebake bake in the oven (bottom rack)
for 10 minutes.

2 | Arrange berries on the cake and bake
for another 15–20 minutes. Stir together
powdered sugar and lemon juice to make
a smooth glaze and pour onto cooled cake.

Mulled Wine Brownies

MAKES 1 JELLYROLL PAN (15 PIECES):

➤ 4 eggs | 1¼ cups sugar | ¾ cup oil
¾ cup mulled wine | 1 heaping
tsp cinnamon | 1 cup grated chocolate
2¼ cups flour | 1 tbs cocoa powder
1 tbs baking powder
1½ cups powdered sugar | 3 tbs rum

1 | Preheat oven to 400°F. Beat eggs and
sugar until light and creamy. Add oil,
mulled wine, 1 level tsp cinnamon, grated
chocolate, and flour mixed with cocoa
and baking powder. Spread out batter
in the prepared pan and bake in the
oven (bottom rack) for 20–25 minutes.

2 | Mix powdered sugar with a little
cinnamon and the rum to make a glaze
and pour onto the cake.

23

Can Prepare in Advance

Cherry Cake

MAKES ONE BAKING
SHEET:

➤ 4 eggs

1¼ cups sugar

¾ cup oil

¾ cup orange juice

1¾ cups grated chocolate

2¼ cups flour

1 tbs baking powder

➤ For the topping
and streusel:

1 jar sour cherries
(12 oz)

1¼ cups butter

3 tbs sugar

1 tsp vanilla

1½ cups flour

🕐 Prep time: 35 minutes

🕐 Baking time: 30 minutes

➤ Calories per piece (25):
About 275

1 | Preheat oven to 400°F.
Beat eggs and sugar until light
and creamy. Add oil, orange
juice, and grated chocolate.
Briskly stir in flour mixed
with baking powder. Spread
out batter in the prepared
pan and prebake in the oven
(bottom rack) for 12 minutes.

2 | In the meantime, drain
cherries. Melt butter, let cool
slightly, and mix with sugar,
vanilla, and flour to make a
crumbly dough. Arrange
cherries on prebaked base
and crumble streusel over the
top. Bake cake for another
15–20 minutes.

Fruity | Easy

Apricot Dollop Cake

MAKES 1 JELLYROLL PAN:

➤ 1 (16-oz) can apricots

4 eggs

1¼ cups sugar

¾ cup oil

2¼ cups flour

1 tbs baking powder

4 tbs poppy seeds

⅓ cup ground hazelnuts

🕐 Prep time: 30 minutes

🕐 Baking time: 30 minutes

➤ Calories per serving (15):
About 285

1 | Preheat oven to 400°F.
Drain apricots, keeping
¾ cup of the juice.

2 | Beat eggs and sugar until
light and creamy. Add oil
and apricot juice. Briskly stir
in flour mixed with baking
powder. Pour half the batter
into the prepared pan. Divide
remaining batter in half. Mix
one half with poppy seeds
and spoon it onto the base
in dollops.

3 | Mix remaining batter with
hazelnuts and dollop it onto
the batter in between the
poppy seed dollops. Prebake
cake base in the oven (bottom
rack) for 5–10 minutes.

4 | Arrange apricots on
prebaked base and bake cake
for another 15–20 minutes.

TIP
Instead of poppy
seeds, you can also
use cocoa powder.

Photo top: **Apricot Dollop Cake**   *Photo bottom:* **Cherry Cake** ➤

Traditional | Moist

Apple Streusel

MAKES 1 JELLYROLL PAN:

- 4 eggs
  1¼ cups sugar
  ¾ cup oil
  ¾ cup white grape juice
  2¼ cups flour
  ½ tsp cinnamon
  1 tbs baking powder
- For the streusel:
  1¼ cup butter
  ½ cup sugar
  1½ cups flour
  1½ tbs cocoa powder
  5 tart apples

🕑 Prep time: 30 minutes
🕑 Baking time: 40 minutes
➤ Calories per piece (15):
  About 395

1 | Preheat oven to 400°F. Melt butter for streusel and mix with sugar, flour, and cocoa powder to make a crumbly dough.

2 | For cake, beat eggs and sugar until light and creamy. Add oil and grape juice. Briskly stir in flour mixed with cinnamon and baking powder.

3 | Spread out batter in the prepared pan and prebake in the oven (bottom rack) for 12 minutes.

4 | In the meantime, peel apples for topping, grate coarsely, and arrange on the prebaked base. Pull off pieces of streusel and distribute them over the apples. Bake cake for another 30 minutes.

Best When Fresh

Currant Sour Cream Cake

MAKES 1 JELLYROLL PAN:

- 4 eggs
  1¼ cups sugar
  ¾ cup oil
  ¾ cup orange juice
  2¼ cups flour
  1 tbs baking powder
- For the topping:
  2 cups sour cream
  3 eggs
  ¼ cup sugar
  3 cups dried red currants

🕑 Prep time: 35 minutes
🕑 Baking time: 45 minutes
➤ Calories per piece (15):
  About 310

1 | Preheat oven to 400°F. Beat eggs and sugar until light and creamy. Add oil and orange juice. Briskly stir in flour mixed with baking powder.

2 | Spread out batter in the prepared pan and prebake in the oven (bottom rack) for 12–15 minutes.

3 | Mix together sour cream, eggs, and sugar and pour mixture onto the prepared base. Distribute currants on top and bake cake for another 25–30 minutes.

Easy

Rhubarb Cake

MAKES 1 JELLYROLL PAN:

➤ 4 eggs
1¼ cups sugar
¾ cup oil
¾ cup carbonated orange drink
2¼ cups flour
3 tbs cocoa powder
1 tbs baking powder
➤ For the topping:
8 stalks rhubarb
2 cups sour cream
4 eggs
⅓ cup sugar

🕐 Prep time: 40 minutes
🕐 Baking time: 35 minutes
➤ Calories per piece (15):
About 325

1 | Preheat oven to 400°F. For the topping, clean rhubarb, peel, and cut into small pieces.

2 | Beat eggs and sugar until light and creamy. Add oil and orange drink. Briskly stir in flour mixed with cocoa powder and baking powder.

3 | Spread out batter in the prepared pan and prebake in the oven (bottom rack) for 15 minutes.

4 | In the meantime, thoroughly mix together sour cream, eggs, and sugar for the topping. Fold in rhubarb.

5 | Distribute rhubarb topping on the prebaked base. Bake cake for another 15–20 minutes.

Fast | Moist

Pear Lattice Cake

MAKES 1 JELLYROLL PAN:

➤ 5 pears
4 eggs
1¼ cups sugar
¾ cup oil
¾ cup pear juice
½ cup sliced almonds
2¼ cups flour
1 tbs baking powder
1 pinch ground cloves
➤ For the topping:
¾ cup semisweet chocolate
2 tbs sliced almonds

🕐 Prep time: 30 minutes
🕐 Baking time: 35 minutes
➤ Calories per piece (15):
About 335

1 | Preheat oven to 400°F. Peel pears, cut into quarters, remove cores, and cut wedges crosswise into fine slices.

2 | Beat eggs and sugar until light and creamy. Add oil and juice and stir in sliced almonds. Briskly stir in flour mixed with baking powder and ground cloves. Fold in pear slices.

3 | Spread out batter in the prepared pan and bake in the oven (bottom rack) for 30–35 minutes.

4 | Melt chocolate in a double boiler and pour into a small freezer bag. Cut off one corner of the bag and let chocolate run onto cake in a lattice pattern. Sprinkle with sliced almonds and let lattice dry.

Aromatic

Chocolate Spice Cake

MAKES 1 JELLYROLL PAN:

➤ 3 oz Nutella
  4 eggs
  1¼ cups brown sugar
  ¾ cup oil
  ½ cup milk
  ¼ cup orange juice
  2¼ cups flour
  1 tsp star anise
  2 tbs cocoa powder
  1 tbs baking powder
  ¾ cup whole peeled almonds

🕓 Prep time: 35 minutes
🕓 Baking time: 25 minutes
➤ Calories per piece (15):
  About 295

1 | Preheat oven to 400°F. Heat Nutella slightly in a double boiler.

2 | Beat eggs and sugar until light and creamy. Add oil, milk, orange juice, and Nutella. Briskly stir in flour mixed with star anise, cocoa, and baking powder.

3 | Spread out batter in the prepared pan and prebake in the oven (bottom rack) for 10–12 minutes.

4 | Distribute almonds over the prebaked base and bake cake for another 15 minutes.

For Gourmets

Walnut Squares

MAKES 1 JELLYROLL PAN:

➤ 1¾ cups walnuts
  4 eggs
  1¼ cups sugar
  ¾ cup oil
  ¾ cup orange juice
  2¼ cups flour
  ½ tsp cinnamon
  1 pinch ground cloves
  1 tbs baking powder
➤ For the glaze and
  decorations:
  1¾ cups powdered sugar
  1 pinch cinnamon
  ¼ cup rum (may substitute orange juice)
  About 15 walnut halves

🕓 Prep time: 35 minutes
🕓 Baking time: 25 minutes
➤ Calories per piece (15):
  About 220

1 | Preheat oven to 400°F. Chop walnuts coarsely.

2 | Beat eggs and sugar until light and creamy. Add oil and juice. Briskly stir in chopped walnuts and flour mixed with spices and baking powder.

3 | Spread out batter in the prepared pan, bake in the oven (bottom rack) for 20–25 minutes, and let cool.

4 | Sift powdered sugar. Add cinnamon and then stir in rum drop by drop to make a smooth, syrupy glaze. Spread glaze onto cake and top with walnut halves.

5 | Let glaze dry and cut cake into squares before serving.

◄ *Photo top:* **Chocolate Spice Cake**   *Photo bottom:* **Walnut Squares**

Simple Cakes, Fancy Tops

Looking for a knock-out cake to impress your guests? Here are some delicious,

simple to prepare bases that are accented with a variety of attractive toppings,

from crunchy, buttery almonds to a sweet duo of strawberries and pears.

Quick Recipes

Butter Cake

MAKES 1 JELLYROLL PAN (15 PIECES):

➤ 1 package vanilla pudding mix
1 cup heavy cream | 4 eggs
2 cups sugar | $^3/_4$ cup oil
$2^1/_4$ cups flour | 1 tbs baking powder
$2^1/_4$ sticks butter | $1^1/_2$ cups sliced
almonds

1 | Preheat oven to 400°F. Combine
pudding mix and cream. Beat eggs and
1 cup sugar until light and creamy. Stir
in oil, pudding-cream mixture, flour,
and baking powder. Spread out batter
in the prepared pan and prebake in the
oven (bottom rack) for 15 minutes.

2 | Melt butter, mix in almonds, and
remaining sugar and spread evenly over
the base. Bake cake for another 15 minutes.

Glazed Blueberry-Pear Cake

MAKES 1 SPRINGFORM PAN (12 PIECES):

➤ 2 eggs | 1 cup sugar | $^1/_2$ cup oil
$^1/_2$ cup juice | $^1/_2$ cup grated chocolate
$1^1/_2$ cups flour | $1^1/_2$ tsp baking powder
1 (16-oz) can pears | 1 pint fresh blue-
berries | 1 tbs honey (if necessary)

1 | Preheat oven to 400°F. Beat eggs and
$^3/_4$ cup sugar until light and creamy. Stir in
oil, juice, chocolate, and flour mixed with
baking powder. Spread out batter in the
prepared pan and bake in the oven (bottom
rack) for 20–25 minutes.

2 | Drain pears and set aside juice. Cut pears
into wedges and arrange on the cake along
with blueberries. Prepare glaze using juice
from pears, remaining sugar, and honey.
Drizzle glaze over the fruit.

33

Fast | Fruity

Kiwi Cake

MAKES 1 SPRINGFORM:

- 2 eggs
  - $2/3$ cup sugar
  - $1/2$ cup oil
  - $1/2$ cup fruit juice
  - $1 1/4$ cups flour
  - $1 1/2$ tbs baking powder
- For the topping and glaze:
  - 8 ripe kiwis
  - Juice from $1/2$ lemon
  - 2 tbs sugar
  - 1 tbs honey

- Prep time: 20 minutes
- Baking time: 25 minutes
- Calories per piece (12): About 165

1 | Preheat oven to 400°F. Beat eggs and sugar until light and creamy. Add oil and juice. Briskly stir in flour mixed with baking powder. Pour batter into the prepared pan, bake in the oven (bottom rack) for 20–25 minutes, and let cool.

2 | Place a tart ring around the cake base. Peel kiwis, slice, and arrange on base. Add water to lemon juice until you have 1 cup. Using this liquid, the sugar, and honey, prepare glaze by heating all three until you have a uniform consistency. Let cool and drizzle over the cake.

TIP Tastes delicious with chocolate-flecked whipped cream (recipe on page 58).

Moist | Easy

Strawberry Pear Cake

MAKES 1 SPRINGFORM PAN:

- 2 eggs
  - $2/3$ cup sugar
  - $1/2$ cup oil
  - 1 cup flour
  - 2 tbs cocoa powder
  - $1 1/2$ tsp baking powder
- For the topping and glaze:
  - 1 large (16-oz) can pears
  - 2 pints strawberries
  - 4 tbs sugar

- Prep time: 25 minutes
- Baking time: 25 minutes
- Calories per piece (12): About 200

1 | Preheat oven to 400°F. For the topping, drain pears. Measure out $1/4$ cup of the juice (and set aside the rest).

2 | Beat eggs and sugar until light and creamy. Add oil and the pear juice. Briskly stir in flour mixed with cocoa powder and baking powder. Pour batter into the prepared pan, bake in the oven (bottom rack) for 20–25 minutes, and let cool.

3 | In the meantime, rinse and dry strawberries, remove stems, and slice. Cut pears into wedges. Place a tart ring around the cooled cake base. Arrange pears around the edge. Arrange strawberries tightly together inside this ring and heap them up a little in the center.

4 | Add water to remaining pear juice until you have 1 cup. Cook this liquid with the sugar until you have a smooth glaze that is thick enough to coat a spoon. Cool glaze a bit and drizzle over the fruit.

Impressive | Fruity

Blood Orange Cake

MAKES 1 SPRINGFORM PAN:

- **2 eggs**
  - $^2/_3$ cup sugar
  - $^1/_2$ cup oil
  - $^1/_2$ cup orange juice
  - $^1/_2$ cup poppy seeds
  - 1 cup flour
  - $1^1/_2$ tsp baking powder
- **For the topping and glaze:**
  - 7 blood oranges
  - 6 tbs sugar
  - 1 cup heavy cream
  - 1 tsp vanilla

⏱ Prep time: 40 minutes

⏱ Baking time: 25 minutes

- **Calories per piece (12):** About 275

1 | Preheat oven to 400°F. Beat eggs and sugar until light and creamy. Add oil and juice. Briskly stir in poppy seeds and flour mixed with baking powder. Pour batter into the prepared pan, bake in the oven (bottom rack) for 25 minutes, and let cool.

2 | Place a tart ring around the cooled cake. Using a sharp knife, peel 5 oranges down to the flesh, cut into thin slices ($^1/_8$ inch), and arrange on the cake. Squeeze juice from remaining oranges and strain juice (if necessary, add water until you have 1 cup). Cook this liquid with 4 tbs sugar until you have a smooth glaze that is thick enough to coat a spoon. Cool glaze a bit and drizzle over the fruit and let cake set.

3 | Beat cream, vanilla, and remaining sugar. Transfer to a pastry bag with a star tip and pipe on cream rosettes around the cake border.

TIP Instead of blood oranges you can, of course, use regular oranges!

1 Slice off bottom of orange evenly.

2 Cut off thick strips of peel from top to bottom.

3 Cut fruit crosswise into slices $^1/_8$-inch thick.

Best When Fresh

Berry Cake

MAKES 1 SPRINGFORM PAN:

- 2 eggs
  $^2/_3$ cup sugar
  $^1/_2$ cup oil
  $^1/_2$ cup orange juice
  1 cup flour
  1 tbs baking powder
- For the topping and glaze:
  1 pint blueberries
  1 pint raspberries
  4 tbs sugar
  2 cups cran-raspberry or
  cran-strawberry juice
  2 tbs slice almonds
  Whipped cream for
  decorating (optional)

- Prep time: 30 minutes
- Baking time: 25 minutes
- Calories per piece (12):
  About 180

1 | Preheat oven to 400°F.
Beat eggs and sugar until light
and creamy. Add oil and juice.
Briskly stir in flour mixed
with baking powder. Pour
batter into the prepared pan,
bake in the oven (bottom
rack) for 20–25 minutes,
and let cool.

2 | Place a tart ring around
the cake base. Arrange berries
on the cake.

3 | Prepare a glaze by heating
the sugar and juice until it is
thick enough to coat a spoon.
Pour glaze over the berries
and let it set. Decorate sides of
cake with sliced almonds and,
if desired, top each slice with
a whipped cream rosette.

Moist | For a Buffet

Plum Cake

MAKES 1 SPRINGFORM
PAN:

- 1 cup walnuts
  2 eggs
  $^2/_3$ cup sugar
  $^1/_2$ cup oil
  $^1/_2$ cup apple juice
  1 cup flour
  1 $^1/_2$ tsp baking powder
- For the topping and glaze:
  6–8 plums (about 1 lb)
  1 cup plum juice
  4 tbs sugar

- Prep time: 35 minutes
- Baking time: 25 minutes
- Calories per piece (12):
  About 235

1 | Preheat oven to 400°F.
Chop walnuts finely.

2 | Beat eggs and sugar until
light and creamy. Add oil and
juice. Briskly stir in walnuts
and flour mixed with baking
powder. Pour batter into the
prepared pan, bake in the
oven (bottom rack) for
20–25 minutes, and let cool.

3 | Place a tart ring around
the cake base. Cut plums
from the pit, dice finely, and
distribute over the cake.
Prepare glaze by slowly
cooking plum juice and the
sugar until it is thick enough
to coat a spoon. Pour over
the plums and let it set.

TIP You can also pipe a
decorative cinnamon
whipped cream lattice
(recipe on page 58)
onto this cake.

Fruity | Fast

Raspberry Cake

MAKES 1 SPRINGFORM PAN:

- 2 eggs
  $^2/_3$ cup sugar
  $^1/_2$ cup oil
  $^1/_2$ cup orange juice
  1 cup flour
  2 tbs cocoa powder
  1 tbs baking powder
- For the topping:
  1 cup cran-raspberry juice
  1 pint raspberries
  6 tbs sugar

⏱ Prep time: 25 minutes
⏱ Baking time: 20 minutes
- Calories per piece (12):
  About 170

1 | Preheat oven to 400°F. Beat eggs and sugar until light and creamy. Add oil and juice. Briskly stir in flour mixed with cocoa powder and baking powder. Pour batter into the prepared pan and bake in the oven (bottom rack) for 20 minutes.

2 | Place a tart ring around the cooled cake base. Prepare glaze by heating juice and sugar until it is thick enough to coat a spoon. Fold in raspberries and distribute mixture over the cake base. Let topping set in the refrigerator.

Easy | For Company

Poppy Seed Cake with Peaches

MAKES 1 SPRINGFORM PAN:

- 2 eggs
  $^2/_3$ cup sugar
  $^1/_2$ cup oil
  $^1/_2$ cup peach juice
  $^1/_2$ cup poppy seeds
  1 cup flour
  $1^1/_2$ tbs baking powder
- For the topping and garnish:
  1 large (16-oz) can peaches
  2 cups heavy cream
  2 tsp vanilla
  4 tbs sugar
  2 tbs grated chocolate

⏱ Prep time: 30 minutes
⏱ Baking time: 30 minutes
- Calories per piece (12):
  About 320

1 | Preheat oven to 400°F. For the topping, drain peaches and measure out $^1/_2$ cup of the juice for the cake.

2 | Beat eggs and sugar until light and creamy. Add oil and peach juice, then mix in poppy seeds. Briskly stir in flour mixed with baking powder. Pour batter into the prepared pan, bake in the oven (bottom rack) for 25–30 minutes, and let cool.

3 | Cut 3 peach halves into thin slices and dice remaining peaches finely. Place a tart ring around the cooled cake.

4 | Beat cream, vanilla, and sugar. Fold in diced peaches and distribute mixture over the base. Arrange peach slices on top and sprinkle with grated chocolate. Refrigerate cake until ready to serve.

Photo top: **Poppy Seed Cake with Peaches**   *Photo bottom:* **Raspberry Cake** ➤

Can Prepare in Advance | Impressive

Hazelnut Cake with Tangerines

MAKES 1 SPRINGFORM PAN:

➤ **4 eggs**
1 ¼ cups sugar
¾ cup oil
¾ cup milk
1 cup grated chocolate
½ cup ground hazelnuts
2 ¼ cups flour
1 tbs baking powder
➤ **For the filling and**
decorations:
3 medium tangerines
2 cups heavy cream
2 tsp vanilla
4 tbs sugar

🕐 Prep time: 35 minutes
🕐 Baking time: 50 minutes
➤ Calories per piece (12):
About 500

1 | Preheat oven to 400°F. Beat eggs and sugar until light and creamy. Add oil and milk. Briskly stir in grated chocolate, hazelnuts, and flour mixed with baking powder. Pour batter into the prepared pan, bake in the oven (bottom rack) for 45–50 minutes, and let cool.

2 | In the meantime, peel tangerines, including the white pith. Set aside several sections for decorating. Hollow out cake with a spoon, leaving a 1-inch border around the edges. Crumble the cake you removed and set aside.

3 | Beat cream, vanilla, and sugar until stiff. Fold in crumbled cake and tangerines and spoon gently into the base.

4 | Decorate cake with the mandarin orange sections you saved and refrigerate until ready to serve.

TIPS

➤ It's easiest to hollow out this cake if you bake it the day before.

➤ This cake looks delicious sprinkled with 1–2 tbs grated chocolate.

1 *Hollow out cooled cake with a spoon.*

2 *Uniformly crumble the cake you removed.*

3 *Fold crumbled cake and tangerine sections into cream.*

Tempting Tortes

Naturally, no book on baking would be complete without tortes—but don't be intimidated, the tortes you'll find here are not complicated. All you need is a little time and patience.

Quick Recipes

Chocolate Cream Torte

MAKES 1 SPRINGFORM PAN (14 PIECES):

➤ 2 eggs | $^2/_3$ cup sugar | $^1/_2$ cup oil
$^1/_2$ cup cappucino | 2 tbs cocoa powder
1 cup flour | $1^1/_2$ tsp baking powder
2 cups heavy cream | 5 tbs chocolate
milk powder | 3 tangerines

1 | Using the basic batter recipe instructions (page 4), make a cake with eggs, sugar, oil, cappuccino, cocoa powder, flour, and baking powder. Bake for 25 minutes, let cool, and cut horizontally into two layers.

2 | Beat cream until stiff, then set aside 5 tbs for garnishing finished cake. Fold in chocolate milk powder and spread onto the bottom layer. Peel tangerines and distribute sections on top of the cream. Cover with the second cake layer. Spread entire cake with chocolate cream and decorate with whipped cream rosettes.

Eggnog Torte

MAKES 1 SPRINGFORM PAN (12 PIECES):

➤ $^3/_4$ cup almonds | 2 eggs | $^3/_4$ cup sugar
$^1/_2$ cup oil | $^1/_2$ cup orange juice
$^1/_2$ cup grated chocolate | 1 cup flour
1 tbs cocoa powder | $1^1/_2$ tsp baking
powder | 2 cups heavy cream
4 tbs eggnog

1 | Grind half the almonds and chop the other half. Using the basic recipe (page 4), make a cake with eggs, $^2/_3$ cup sugar, oil, juice, grated chocolate, ground and chopped almonds, flour, cocoa powder, and baking powder. Bake for 25–30 minutes and let cool.

2 | Beat cream and remaining sugar until stiff, then set aside 5 tbs for garnishing finished cake. Spread whipped cream onto base. Using the 5 tbs of remaining whipped cream, pipe rosettes around the border and drizzle eggnog in the center.

45

For Special Occasions
Hazelnut Cream Torte

MAKES 1 SPRINGFORM PAN:

- 4 eggs
  1¼ cups sugar
  ¾ cup oil
  ¾ cup milk
  2 cups ground hazelnuts
  2¼ cups flour
  1 tbs baking powder
- For the filling:
  5 tbs blackberry jam
  2½ cups heavy cream
  1 tbs vanilla
  6 tbs sugar
  14 whole hazelnuts

- Prep time: 30 minutes
- Baking time: 50 minutes
- Calories per piece (14): About 550

1 | Preheat oven to 400°F. Beat eggs and sugar until light and creamy. Add oil and milk. Stir in ⅔ of the hazelnuts and flour mixed with baking powder. Pour batter into the prepared pan and bake in the oven (bottom rack) for 45–50 minutes.

2 | Cut cake horizontally into three layers. Spread jam onto bottom layer and place middle layer on top of jam. Beat cream, vanilla, and sugar until stiff and place 5 tbs in a pastry bag with a star tip.

3 | Mix remaining ground hazelnuts into the cream that is not in the pastry bag. Spread one-third onto the middle layer, place third cake layer on top, and frost the entire torte with the last of the hazelnut cream. Pipe whipped cream rosettes around the border and top each rosette with a whole hazelnut.

Can Prepare in Advance
Lemon Cream Torte

MAKES 1 SPRINGFORM PAN:

- 4 eggs
  1¼ cups sugar
  ¾ cup oil
  ¾ cup orange juice
  Juice from 1 lemon
  2¼ cups flour
  1 tbs baking powder
- For the filling:
  3 lemons
  2½ cups heavy cream
  ½ cup sugar
  1 tbs vanilla
  3 tbs currant jelly

- Prep time: 40 minutes
- Baking time: 50 minutes
- Calories per piece (14): About 385

1 | Preheat oven to 400°F. Beat eggs and sugar until light and creamy. Add oil, orange juice, and lemon juice. Briskly stir in flour mixed with baking powder. Pour batter into the prepared pan and bake in the oven (bottom rack) for 45–50 minutes.

2 | Squeeze juice from all but ½ lemon and slice the remaining lemon half into ⅛-inch pieces. Beat cream, sugar, and vanilla until stiff and stir in lemon juice.

3 | Cut cake horizontally into three layers. Spread jelly onto bottom layer and place middle layer on top of jelly. Spread middle layer with one-third of the lemon cream and place third layer on top.

4 | Place 4 tbs lemon cream in a pastry bag with a star tip. Frost the entire torte with the remaining cream. Pipe on cream rosettes around the border, cut up lemon slices, and place one piece on top of each rosette.

For Gourmets | Impressive

Chocolate Strawberry Torte

MAKES 1 SPRINGFORM PAN:

➤ **4 eggs**
  1¼ cups sugar
  ¾ cup oil
  ¾ cup orange juice
  2¼ cups flour
  1 tbs baking powder
➤ **For the filling and decorations:**
  2 cups semisweet chocolate couverture
  2 pints strawberries
  3½ cups heavy cream
  2 tbs vanilla
  ½ cup sugar
  Grated chocolate for sprinkling (optional)

🕐 Prep time: 60 minutes
🕐 Baking time: 40 minutes
➤ Calories per piece (14): About 550

1 | Preheat oven to 400°F. Beat eggs and sugar until light and creamy. Add oil and juice. Stir in flour mixed with baking powder. Pour batter into the prepared pan, bake in the oven (bottom rack) for 35–40 minutes, and let cool.

2 | Melt couverture in a double boiler. Rinse strawberries and drain. For the decorations, cut 10 nice strawberries with stems in half lengthwise and dip each half partway into the melted couverture. Place on a piece of aluminum foil to dry. Remove stems from remaining strawberries. Purée half these berries and chop the other half.

3 | Cut cake horizontally into three layers. Spread couverture onto bottom and middle layers and let harden.

4 | Beat cream, vanilla, and sugar until stiff. Mix half the cream with strawberry purée. Spread half of the strawberry cream onto the bottom layer. Place middle layer on top, spread with remaining strawberry cream, and sprinkle with chopped strawberries. Place third layer on top.

5 | Frost the entire torte with the plain whipped cream. Decorate with chocolate-covered strawberries and grated chocolate, if desired.

1 *Melt couverture in a double boiler.*

2 *Dip strawberry halves partway into chocolate.*

3 *Place strawberries on aluminum foil and let chocolate harden.*

Cranberry Torte

MAKES 1 SPRINGFORM PAN:

- **2 eggs**
  ³/₄ cup sugar
  ¹/₂ cup oil
  ¹/₂ cup orange juice
  ¹/₂ cup ground hazelnuts
  ¹/₂ cup grated chocolate
  1 cup flour
  1¹/₂ tsp baking powder
  1¹/₂ tbs gelatin
  4 cups yogurt
  1¹/₄ cups cranberries
  2 cups heavy cream
  Cocoa powder for dusting

- Prep time: 40 minutes
- Baking time: 30 minutes
- Refrigeration time: 5 hours
- Calories per piece (12):
  About 405

1 | Preheat oven to 400°F.
Beat eggs and ¹/₂ cup sugar
until light and creamy.
Add oil and juice. Briskly
stir in hazelnuts, grated
chocolate, and flour mixed
with baking powder.

2 | Pour batter into the
prepared pan, bake in the
oven (bottom rack) for 20–25
minutes, and let cool.

3 | Soak gelatin. Place a tart
ring around the cake. Stir
together yogurt and cran-
berries until smooth. Dissolve
gelatin over low heat, add
1–2 tbs of the yogurt mixture,
and then stir into yogurt. Let
set in the refrigerator.

4 | Beat cream with remaining
sugar until stiff and fold into
yogurt cream. Spread the
mixture onto the cake base
and refrigerate for 5 hours.
Dust with cocoa powder
before serving.

Banana Cream Torte

MAKES 1 SPRINGFORM PAN:

- **2 eggs**
  ²/₃ cup sugar
  ¹/₂ cup oil
  ¹/₂ cup tart cherry juice
  1 cup flour
  2 tbs cocoa powder
  1¹/₂ tsp baking powder
  2 ¹/₂ cups heavy cream
  5 tbs chocolate milk powder
  3 bananas
  1 tsp vanilla
  2 tbs sugar
  2 tbs grated chocolate
  3 tbs lemon juice

- Prep time: 40 minutes
- Baking time: 25 minutes
- Calories per piece (12):
  About 340

1 | Preheat oven to 400°F.
Beat eggs and sugar until light
and creamy. Add oil and juice.
Briskly stir in flour mixed
with cocoa powder and
baking powder. Pour batter
into the prepared pan, bake
in the oven (bottom rack) for
20–25 minutes, and let cool.

2 | Place a tart ring around
the cake. Beat 2 cups cream
until stiff, then stir in chocolate
milk powder. Peel 2 bananas,
slice, and stir into cream.
Distribute banana chocolate
cream on the base.

3 | Beat remaining cream
with vanilla and sugar until
stiff and distribute over the
chocolate cream. Sprinkle
with grated chocolate. Peel
remaining banana, slice,
drizzle with lemon juice,
and arrange on the torte.
Refrigerate torte until ready
to serve.

Photo top: **Banana Cream Torte**   *Photo bottom:* **Cranberry Torte**

Traditional | Moist

Black Forest Cherry Torte

MAKES 1 SPRINGFORM PAN:

➤ **4 eggs**
1¼ cups sugar
¾ cup oil
¾ cup orange juice
2¼ cups flour
3 tbs cocoa powder
1 tbs baking powder
9 tbs cherry brandy
(may substitute cherry
juice) for drizzling

➤ **For the cherry filling:**
1 large jar sour cherries
(about 14 oz)
1 tbs honey
2 tbs sugar
2 tbs cherry brandy
(optional)

➤ **For the cream filling**
and decorations:
2½ cups heavy cream
3 tsp vanilla
6 tbs sugar
Grated semisweet
chocolate for sprinkling

🕐 Prep time: 50 minutes
🕐 Baking time: 45 minutes
🕐 Refrigeration time: 12 hours
➤ Calories per piece (14):
About 430

1 | Preheat oven to 400°F. Beat eggs and sugar until light and creamy. Add oil and orange juice. Briskly stir in flour mixed with cocoa powder and baking powder.

2 | Pour batter into the prepared pan, bake in the oven (bottom rack) for 40–45 minutes, and let cool.

3 | Cut cake horizontally into three layers. Place a tart ring around the bottom layer and drizzle with 3 tbs cherry brandy.

4 | For the cherry filling, drain sour cherries and set aside the juice. Set aside 14 cherries for decoration.

5 | Prepare fruit glaze by simmering 1 cup of the cherry juice you saved (add water to make 1 cup, if needed), honey, and sugar to a smooth consistency. Stir in cherries that were not set aside and cherry brandy. Distribute this

mixture on the bottom cake layer. Place the middle layer on top and drizzle with 3 tbs cherry brandy.

6 | Beat ⅓ of the cream with 1 tsp vanilla and 2 tbs sugar until stiff and spread onto the middle layer. Place the top layer of cake on the whipped cream, pierce several times, and drizzle with 3 tbs cherry brandy. Refrigerate torte for several hours (preferably overnight).

7 | Carefully remove tart ring. Beat remaining cream, vanilla, and sugar until stiff and use two-thirds to frost the entire torte. Place remaining cream in a pastry bag with a star tip.

8 | Sprinkle the sides of the torte with grated chocolate. Pipe cream rosettes around the border and top each rosette with 1 cherry. Refrigerate torte until ready to serve.

For Gourmets

Tiramisu Torte

MAKES 1 SPRINGFORM PAN:

- 4 eggs
  1$\frac{1}{4}$ cups sugar
  $\frac{3}{4}$ cup oil
  $\frac{3}{4}$ cup orange juice
  3 tbs cocoa powder
  2$\frac{1}{4}$ cups flour
  1 tbs baking powder
  3 cups mascarpone
  3 egg yolks
  1 tbs vanilla
  2 tbs sugar
  $\frac{1}{2}$ cup espresso
  $\frac{1}{4}$ cup amaretto
  Cocoa powder for dusting

- Prep time: 45 minutes
- Baking time: 45 minutes
- Calories per piece (14): About 550

1 | Preheat oven to 400°F. Beat eggs and sugar until light and creamy. Add oil and juice. Briskly stir in flour mixed with cocoa powder and baking powder. Pour batter into the prepared pan and bake in the oven (bottom rack) for 40–45 minutes.

2 | Cut cake horizontally into three layers. Beat together mascarpone, egg yolks, vanilla, and sugar until spreadable. Mix espresso and amaretto and drizzle bottom cake layer with 5 tbs of espresso mixture. Top with a thin layer of mascarpone cream and place the middle layer on top. Again drizzle with espresso mixture and spread with a thin layer of mascarpone cream. Place third layer on top, pierce several times, and again drizzle with espresso mixture.

3 | Frost the entire torte with the remaining mascarpone cream and refrigerate. Dust with cocoa powder just before serving.

Easy

Nougat Torte

MAKES 1 SPRINGFORM PAN:

- 4 eggs
  $\frac{1}{2}$ cup sugar
  $\frac{3}{4}$ cup oil
  $\frac{3}{4}$ cup milk
  1$\frac{1}{4}$ cups ground hazelnuts
  2$\frac{1}{4}$ cups flour
  1 tbs baking powder
- For the filling and frosting:
  $\frac{3}{4}$ cup honey
  $\frac{3}{4}$ cup chopped, roasted hazelnuts
  2 egg whites
  2$\frac{1}{2}$ cups cream
  4 tbs chocolate milk powder

- Prep time: 40 minutes
- Baking time: 35 minutes
- Calories per piece (14): About 510

1 | Preheat oven to 400°F. Beat eggs and sugar until light and creamy. Add oil and milk. Briskly stir in hazelnuts and flour mixed with baking powder. Pour batter into the prepared pan and bake in the oven (bottom rack) for 30–35 minutes.

2 | Cut cake horizontally into three layers. Heat honey and hazelnuts over low heat. Beat egg whites until stiff and fold into hazelnuts. Spread one-half of this nougat mixture onto the bottom layer. Place the middle layer on top.

3 | Beat cream until stiff, placing 5 tbs in a pastry bag with a star tip. Stir chocolate milk powder into remaining cream. Spread middle layer with part of the chocolate cream. Place the third layer on top and spread with remaining hazelnut-nougat. Frost the entire cake with chocolate cream and decorate with whipped cream rosettes.

◀ *Photo top:* **Nougat Torte**   *Photo bottom:* **Tiramisu Torte**

Aromatic | For a Buffet
Marzipan Torte

MAKES 1 SPRINGFORM PAN:

➤ 1¼ cups walnuts | 4 eggs
½ cup sugar | ¾ cup oil
¾ cup orange juice
2¼ cups flour
1 tbs baking powder
4 tbs elderberry jam (may substitute blackberry)
2½ cups heavy cream
2 pinches cinnamon
14 oz marzipan
1 cup powdered sugar
1 tsp rum (optional)
Cinnamon, cocoa powder and powdered sugar

🕐 Prep time: 60 min.
🕐 Baking time: 50 minutes
➤ Calories per piece (14): About 595

1 | Preheat oven to 400°F. Chop walnuts finely. Beat eggs and sugar until light and creamy. Stir in oil, juice, walnuts, and flour mixed with baking powder. Pour batter into the prepared pan and bake in the oven (bottom rack) for 45–50 minutes.

2 | Cut cooled cake horizontally into three layers. Spread bottom layer with jam and place the middle layer on top. Beat cream and cinnamon until stiff and spread onto middle layer.

3 | Knead together marzipan, powdered sugar, and rum. Divide mixture in half and roll out each half between two sheets of wax paper to the size of the springform pan. Place one sheet on top of the layer of cream. Place the third cake layer on top, spread with cream, and top with the second marzipan sheet. Spread cinnamon cream around the sides of the torte. Pipe on remaining cream as small rosettes around the border. Sift cinnamon, cocoa powder, and powdered sugar over the top.

Traditional
For Special Occasions
Vanilla Hazelnut Wreath

MAKES 1 TUBE PAN:

➤ 4 eggs | 1¼ cups sugar
¾ cup oil
¾ cup orange juice
2¼ cups flour
1 tbs baking powder
1 package vanilla pudding mix
2 cups milk
1 cup butter at room temperature
1 cup powdered sugar
5 tbs strawberry jam
¾ cup chopped hazelnuts

🕐 Prep time: 60 min.
🕐 Baking time: 45 minutes
➤ Calories per piece (15): About 545

1 | Preheat oven to 400°F. Beat eggs and sugar until light and creamy. Stir in oil, juice, and flour mixed with baking powder. Pour batter into the prepared pan and bake in the oven (bottom rack) for 40–45 minutes.

2 | Combine pudding mix and milk. Beat butter and powdered sugar until creamy. Beat in pudding. Place 4 tbs of this butter cream in a pastry bag.

3 | Cut cooled cake horizontally into three layers. Spread bottom layer with jam, place the middle layer on top, and spread with buttercream. Place third layer on top and frost entire wreath with buttercream. Sprinkle hazelnuts on top and pipe on buttercream rosettes.

Whipped Cream, Please!

Variations on a Theme

Whipped cream is the crown jewel of many a cake. But who would have thought that this white, airy, sweet substance could be so versatile? Here is an entire spectrum of possibilities for refining your whipped cream by giving it a delicious flavor and an attractive color.

Here's How

Use only fresh, chilled heavy whipping cream. If the surroundings are too warm, the cream won't get stiff. So on a hot or muggy day, refrigerate the mixing bowl and wire whisk as well as the cream before beating. If necessary, you can sit the bowl in a larger bowl filled with ice water as you beat the cream.

Whipped cream will stay firm for a long time if you beat in 1 packet of whipped cream stabilizer for each cup of cream. This is especially advisable for the fillings in cream tortes.

In the Recipe Section

The following whipped cream variations are described in the recipe section. You can alter the amounts and proportions of the ingredients listed as needed.

Peach whipped cream—page 40
Tangerine whipped cream—page 43
Chocolate whipped cream—page 45
Lemon whipped cream—page 46
Hazelnut whipped cream— page 46
Strawberry whipped cream—page 49

Tangy Whipped Cream

Good on Fruit Bases
1 cup heavy cream
1 tsp vanilla
1 tbs sugar
1 cup sour cream

Beat cream, vanilla, and sugar until stiff and fold in sour cream.

Chocolate-Flecked Whipped Crea

Delicious with fruity cakes

1 cup heavy cream

1 tsp vanilla

2 tbs sugar

3 tbs grated chocolate

Beat cream, vanilla, and sugar until stiff and fold in grated chocolate.

Cinnamon Whipped Cream

Tasty with apple and plum cakes

1 cup heavy cream

1 tsp vanilla

2 tbs sugar

1–2 pinches cinnamon

Beat cream, vanilla, and sugar until stiff while sprinkling in cinnamon.

Nougat Whipped Cream

A creamy delight
1 tbs honey
1 tbs chopped, roasted hazelnuts
1 cup heavy cream

Heat honey and hazelnuts over low heat. Beat cream until stiff and fold in hazelnut-nougat.

Banana Whipped Cream

Ideal for simple batter cakes
1 banana
1 tbs lemon juice
1 cup heavy cream
3 tbs chocolate milk powder

Peel banana, slice, and drizzle with lemon juice. Beat cream until stiff, stir in chocolate powder, and fold in bananas.

Mocha Whipped Cream

For those who like it bittersweet
1 cup heavy cream
1 tsp vanilla
2 tbs sugar
3 tbs cold, strong coffee

Beat cream, vanilla, and sugar until stiff and stir in cold coffee one spoonful at a time.

Orange Whipped Cream

Wonderful with nut and chocolate cakes
1 cup heavy cream
1 tsp vanilla
2 tbs sugar
Juice from $\frac{1}{2}$ orange

Beat cream, vanilla, and sugar until stiff and stir in orange juice one spoonful at a time.

Almond Whipped Cream

Whipped cream that goes "crunch"
1 cup heavy cream
1 tsp vanilla
2 tbs sugar
2–3 tbs sliced almonds

Beat cream, vanilla, and sugar until stiff and fold in sliced almonds.

Raspberry Whipped Cream

Great with thawed, frozen raspberries
1 cup heavy cream
1 tsp vanilla
2 tbs sugar
3 tbs strained raspberry purée

Beat cream, vanilla, and sugar until stiff and fold in raspberry purée.

TIME INFORMATION
The prep times specified
in these recipes refer only
to the time you're actively
working and include
the time necessary for
preparing the ingredients
and tools, for making the
batter, and for putting
together the cake. They
do not include baking
or any cooling or
refrigeration times.

ABBREVIATIONS

lb = pound
oz = ounce
tsp = teaspoon
tbs = tablespoon

The Author

Gina Greifenstein lives with her family in the southern Palatinate region of Germany. She's very much at home in the world of books—in addition to her job in a bookstore, she has also made a career as an author of short mysteries, children's books and cookbooks. As part of her training as a state-certified home economist, she learned cooking and cake-baking from the ground up. This, along with a large measure of creativity, forms the basis for her recipes. The idea for this book came to her when she developed an easy and uncomplicated marble cake recipe and said, "You could do a whole lot more with this same batter." And she did!

The Photographer

After completing his studies at a photography school in Berlin, Michael Brauner first worked as an assistant to renowned photographers in France and Germany before striking out on his own in 1984. His individual, atmospheric style is highly valued, both in advertising and by many well-known publishers. In his studio in Karlsruhe, he takes photos that bring to life many of the recipes in this and other cookbooks.

Photo Credits

FoodPhotographie Eising, Martina Görlach: cover photo
All others: Michael Brauner, Karlsruhe

Published originally under the title *1 Teig – 50 Kuchen: backen nach Lust und Laune* © 2002 Gräfe und Unzer Verlag GmbH, Munich. English translation for the North America market © 2003, Silverback Books, Inc.

Editors: Jonathan Silverman, Stefanie Poziombka
Translator: Christie Tam
Reader: Claudia Schmidt
Proofreaders: Elizabeth Penn, Susanne Elbert
Typesetting and production: Patty Holden, Verlagssatz Lingner, Helmut Giersberg

Layout, typography and cover design: Independent Medien Design, Munich

Printed in Korea

ISBN 1-930603-42-8

Editions: 5th (2006) 4th (2005), 3rd (2004), 2nd (2003), 1st (2002)

Enjoy Other Quick & Easy Books

Marlisa Szwillus

Fondue

Cheese, vegetable, & all kinds of meat—cook them all right at the table. More than 50 recipes

Cornelia Adam

Salads

Sandwiches

Xenia Burgtorf

Cornelia Adam

Quiche

Delicious, savory pies with vegetables, meat, poultry, fish—serve for all occasions

Cornelia Adam

Garlic

Sophisticated Recipes with the Favorite Spice of the Mediterranean Region. Spicy (tangy), Fine (delicate), International

Cornelia Schinhari

Easy Vegetarian

Uncomplicated and sophisticated — Vegetarian recipes for all seasons

Sebastian Dickhaut

Casseroles

Annette Heisch

Oil & Vinegar

A wonderful source of information, delicious recipes and helpful hints— liven up your favorite dishes and create tasty sauces and dressings

Andreas Fürtmayr

Sushi

Classic ideas from Japan and new fusion sushi. Home-made perfectly.

1 Noodle, 50 Sauces

Everyday Pasta • Old and New Italian Dishes Noodle biography • 10 Tips for Success

Elisabeth Döpp
Christian Willrich
Joerg Rehbe...

Healthy Wok

Great for light and satisfying meals

Antje Gruener

Grilling

Crisp, flavorful and delectable morsels from the grill for your whole family, from spareribs to skewered vegetables, with sauces and chutneys

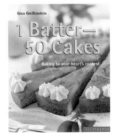

Gina Greifenstein

1 Batter— 50 Cakes

Baking to your heart's content

Cooking in Clay

Healthy Recipes with Great Flavor

Erika Casparek-Türkkan

Doris Muliar

Cocktails for Drivers

100% Enjoyment

Annette Heisch

Antipasti and Tapas

Mediterranean Appetizers
Cornelia Schinhari

Soups

Classic to Contemporary

Sebastian Dickhaut

Claudia Schmidt

Raclette

New Recipes with Cheese, Primer and Party Dips

BASIC INGREDIENTS

- Use only the freshest eggs and dairy products, especially whipping cream.
- If you buy nuts already ground, don't store them too long because they'll quickly turn rancid.

Guaranteed Perfect Cakes

TEMPERATURE

- Be sure to preheat an electric oven far enough in advance. Depending on the manufacturer, this can take 10–20 minutes.
- You don't have to preheat a gas or convection oven because they reach the desired temperature much more rapidly.

TIME SAVERS

- You can bake the base for tortes the day before. This will save you time the next day, and it'll be much easier to cut the cake into layers after it sits overnight.
- You can also save time and electricity by baking two or more cakes in a row and freezing some of them (see Tip 10).

PREPARING BUTTERCREAM

- To keep buttercream from separating when you prepare it, make sure all the ingredients are at room temperature.
- If the buttercream does separate, you can rescue it as follows: Place the cream in a pot, place the pot in a warm double boiler and beat with an electric hand mixer.